What's cooking?

# Late Night Cuisine

## LIGHT EVENING MEALS

# Contents

# Late Night Cuisine

*The later it is the bigger the appetite. Dinner – especially for those who are not at home during the day and who might live off canteen-food or fast-food – is the first and only proper meal of the day. As such it deserves to be enjoyed in its own good time. The following pages will show you all the great things Late Night Cuisine has to offer without being heavy on the stomach or creating digestive problems. The days when you could not go to sleep because of rich food have gone. And the diet that tells you to skip your evening meal is on the wrong track: you do not have to go to bed hungry any more!*

**Light Evening Meals**
It is time to call it a day at work. You pack up your things and prepare to go home. Not long now before your stomach starts rumbling...

The dilemma of many people who work a nine to five day every day is that the evening is their first chance to have a proper meal including everything that goes along with it – enjoyment, peace and relaxation. If you get the chance to eat anything at all during the day, it is likely to be the same old canteen food, sandwiches, crisps and chocolate or the not very satisfying fast-food. All of the above are not what one would call healthy.

**Fit Instead of Fat**
As always, a balanced diet starts with the head, not with the stomach. Forget everything you have ever read about diets that are supposed to work within a week. Banish from your mind all images of starved supermodels or ridiculously fit beach boys. Think a tad further: the most important thing is to feel well! Be moderate, but only in moderation! Those who misunderstand a dietary plan end up not only with less fat, but also with less nutrients. As a result you end up with an unhealthy diet that is not complimentary to body and soul. Inadvertently this leads to frustration and a bad mood which can only be alleviated by a bar of chocolate, a beer and a large bag of crisps. At the end of the day it leads to that well known vicious circle...

Get in shape again and scare the living daylight out of your surplus ounces and pounds. Baroque opulence had its day and you can get rid of it quite easily by applying some common sense rules and by simply watching what you eat. Of course, willpower is part of the equation! Let us be honest: do you not prefer those fatty chips to a green salad? In a restaurant, do you not forego the pleasures of a lean piece of fish in order to feast on a steak? And what about sport? Wonderful thing, as long as it is on the telly...

You can look at it from whichever side you wish – you have to get active in order to get to grips with surplus fat and attain a positive attitude towards your own body. Your ideal weight is not available on prescription nor achievable within fourteen days. It is much more a continuous process that will get you there slowly but surely.

Rule number one: **exercise**. Sitting in the office eight hours a day, taking lifts and escalators, and on top a couch potato in the evening – all this is not going to contribute to having a great figure. Instead your body is under the impression that it does not have to do much and stores energy rather than burning it. Anything you add is going straight to your bum, stomach or hips. And who can blame your body? However, all that is needed is a minimum of regular exercise in order to burn up those calories – to shake off those extra pounds. If possible, take the bike instead of the car. Opt for the stairs rather than the lift, go and take a walk – and do so regularly. Incorporate some exercise into your everyday life. And once you got used it, once you actually enjoy it, think of going jogging, cycling or swimming. Thirty minutes exercise three times a week will work absolute wonders. You will see how quickly regular exercise improves your sense of well-being!

Rule number two: a **balanced** and **healthy diet.** Foods such as vegetables, potatoes, rice, pasta, bread and other cereal products provide you with so-called complex carbohydrates in the form of starch. Furthermore, they blow away your hunger and appetite and are the ideal energy source for exercise and bodily functions. Roughly 60 percent of our daily energy intake should consist of carbohydrates. However, it is only too common that carbohydrates make way for fatty foods. With that in mind you should be aware of what is on your plate. Reduce the fatty stuff and eat more carbohydrates instead.

**Things Are Easier With a Little Roughage**
Of course, quantity alone will not do. You also have to look at the quality of the carbohydrates. There are three

basic kinds: monosaccharides or single sugars, disaccharides or double sugars and complex or multiple saccharides. The first group is comprised among others of glucose, fructose and lactose. Our normal everyday sugar that is used in industrial production processes for sweets and soft drinks belongs to this group. This type of sugar causes the sugar level in the blood to rise rapidly, only for it to fall just as quickly when the sugar is used up. This sudden drop will cause a new hunger attack and you will check your drawers for that second chocolate bar before you know it. Disaccharides or complex saccharides on the other hand behave differently. Because of their complexity the energy they contain is released much slower with the result that you feel full for longer!

Bearing this in mind you should try to reduce your intake of sweets and soft drinks with a lot of sugar and instead concentrate on foods with lots of vitamins, minerals and roughage. Roughage? Be careful not to misunderstand the word and take it literally. They are not rough at all! Wholemeal products such as oats, brown rice, muesli and of course other foods like vegetables, fruit, pulses and, to a certain degree, nuts do not only taste great. They also go a long way to achieving a balanced and healthy diet. This is partly because of the long lasting effect of feeling satisfied after a meal and partly because these foods stimulate the intestines.

**The Later the Evening...**

It is actually quite easy to eat healthily. Shame on us then that we almost always eat too much fatty, sweet and salty foods. But even the most unhealthy Big Mac could be made far less damaging to one's system if we only wanted to (see our chapter "For the Small Appetite").

It is not only the quality of the food we consume, it is also the rhythm, i.e. when, how regularly and how much that plays a very important role. You should always and at all cost avoid attacks of ravenousness. Stuffing yourself or eating far too much overtaxes your metabolism. Instead you should get used to eating less more often during the day. This will make you feel nicely satisfied and prevent such attacks from happening in the first place. Apart from a well balanced breakfast and lunch we recommend a fresh second breakfast consisting of fruit, yoghurt and muesli. On top of that a healthy snack in the afternoon in the form of kefir, buttermilk or fruit will help you overcome the long hours until the evening. Then there is dinner. This should never be the main meal, anyway. A good rule of thumb is that supper should account for about a quarter of your daily intake. Unfortunately, the trend is very much different: dinner is the main meal and worse, it is eaten later and later. For those at work during the day or eating out in the evening this is a more or less unavoidable fact of life. However, you should try to have dinner as early as possible. The best time would be between half past five and six o'clock, seven o'clock at the very latest. The reason? Your metabolism slows down in the evening and instead of burning fatty acids your body starts storing them.

You can avoid this accumulation of fat. All you have to do is eat a dinner which has less fat and proteins and more vegetables and wholemeal products. Our recipes – to serve four – will help you get your evening meals right. Moreover, they should encourage you to enjoy the remains of the day.

...And when you can stand it no more and that bag of crisps or that bar of chocolate is crying out for your attention we say: attack is the best form of defence. Take a walk, get out and have a nice evening stroll to get in your daily exercise. That way you will not only escape temptation but it will also help you unwind after a long day's work.

# For the Small Appetite

*If all you are after is a snack then we have a few fancy recipes in store for you: it only takes a couple of minutes to make a sandwich, a burger, a toast or French stick to nibble on while relaxing in front of the television or reading a good book.*

# Croque Monsieur

***1 bunch chives***

***1 bunch parsley***

***2 cloves of garlic***

***1 1/2 oz (40 g) butter***

***salt***

***pepper***

***2 French rolls***

***8 slices cold roast pork***

***1 tbsp grainy mustard***

***8 oz (250 g) sauerkraut***

***watercress for decoration***

*Preparation time: approx. 20 minutes*
*Per serving: approx. 389 cals/1636 kj*

**1** Preheat the oven to gas mark 4 (350° F or 180° C). Wash, dry and finely chop the herbs. Peel and crush the cloves of garlic.

**2** Work the herbs and the garlic into the butter and season well with salt and pepper. Slice the French rolls in half and spread on the herb butter.

**3** Place the slices of cold roast pork on the herb butter and spread on the mustard. Drain the sauerkraut and place on top of the meat. Cover with top half of the French roll.

**4** Put in the centre of the oven and leave to heat up for approximately 8 minutes. Prior to serving garnish with watercress.

*Mustard is one of the oldest seasonings of all. Already the ancient Greeks knew of its aromatic qualities. The nearly 100 different kinds of mustard all find their origins in the black and white mustard seeds. It is the variety of totally different ingredients that lend each kind of mustard its individual taste and spiciness.*

# Dutch Fish Snack

***2 gherkins***

***2 tbsp orange marmalade***

***cayenne pepper***

***1/2 lollo bianco lettuce***

***4 wholemeal bread rolls***

***4 fillets of plaice (7 oz/200 g each)***

***lemon juice***

***salt***

***freshly milled black pepper***

***2 tbsp olive oil***

*Preparation time: approx. 20 minutes*
*Per serving: approx. 358 cals/1506 kj*

**1** Drain and dice the gherkins. Heat the marmalade in a pan and season with cayenne pepper and 2 tablespoons of gherkin liquid.

**2** Stir in the diced gherkins. Wash and dry the lettuce. Slice open the rolls and garnish with the lettuce leaves. Wash and dry the fillets of plaice and sprinkle with the lemon juice. Season with salt and pepper.

**3** Heat the olive oil in a frying pan and add the fish. Fry for approximately 5 minutes before transferring the fish onto the rolls. Spread on the orange and gherkin sauce. Crown with the top half of the rolls and serve.

# French Stick Hawaii

***3 1/2 oz (100 g) tinned pineapple slices***

***4 French rolls***

***1 1/2 oz (40 g) peanut butter***

***2 tbsp soy sauce***

***ground ginger***

***3 1/2 oz (100 g) cold cooked breast of chicken***

***3 1/2 oz (100 g) celery sticks***

***3 oz (80 g) soft goat's cheese***

*Preparation time: approx. 20 minutes*
*Per serving: approx. 526 cals/2209 kj*

**1** Preheat the oven to gas mark 4 (350° F or 180° C). Place a sieve over a bowl and drain the pineapple. Keep the liquid. Cut open the rolls.

**2** Mix together the soy sauce, peanut butter and 2 fl oz (50 ml) of pineapple liquid. Season with ground ginger. Spread on the bottom halves of the rolls.

**3** Place the cold chicken breast on top of the mixture. Wash and cut the celery into small pieces. Cut the pineapple slices into small pieces, too.

**4** Transfer the celery and the pineapple pieces onto the rolls. Slice the goat's cheese and place on top of the rolls. Put in the centre of the oven and bake for approximately 8 minutes.

# Nuremberg Hot Dog

*1 bunch spring onions*

*4 cornichons*

*2 tbsp olive oil*

*5 oz (150 g) chopped tomatoes*

*2 fl oz (50 ml) white wine*

*salt, pepper, paprika*

*2 tbsp sweet mustard*

*3 tbsp butter*

*8 Nuremberg style frying sausages*

*4 slices toasted wholemeal bread*

*4 lettuce leaves*

*chives for decoration*

*Preparation time: approx. 20 minutes*
*Per serving: approx. 394 cals/1654 kj*

**1** Wash and dry the spring onions and cut into rings. Drain the cornichons and cut into small pieces.

**2** Heat the olive oil in a frying pan and sauté the spring onions and cornichons. Add the chopped tomatoes and white wine and season with salt, pepper, paprika and mustard.

**3** Melt the butter in a second frying pan and brown the sausages for approximately 4 minutes. Place the lettuce leaves on the slices of toasts and top with the fried sausages.

**4** Spread the tomato mixture on top, decorate with chives and serve.

# Rosemary Burger

***4 frozen hamburgers***

***2 onions***

***20 green olives***

***1 sprig rosemary***

***2 tbsp oil***

***salt***

***pepper***

***paprika***

***3 tomatoes***

***1/2 cucumber***

***4 small hamburger baps***

***1 tbsp herb butter***

*Preparation time: approx. 20 minutes*
*Per serving: approx. 898 cals/3771 kj*

**1** Defrost the meat following the instructions on the packet. Peel the onions and cut into rings. Drain and halve the olives.

**2** Chop the rosemary. Heat the oil in a frying pan and brown the burgers on both sides. Add the olives and rosemary and leave to cook for approximately 5 minutes.

**3** Season with salt, pepper and paprika. Wash, dry and slice the tomatoes. Wash and thinly slice the cucumber.

**4** Spread the herb butter on the bottom halves of the baps and place a hamburger on top. Pile on the tomatoes, cucumber pieces and olives. Cover with the top halves and serve.

# Mexico-Burger

***13 oz (400 g) breast of turkey***

***5 tbsp ready made hot salsa***

***2 oz (50 g) tortilla crisps***

***1/2 bunch coriander***

***4 red onions***

***1 clove of garlic***

***salt***

***cayenne pepper***

***caraway seeds***

***3 tbsp sunflower oil***

***4 hamburger baps***

***4 lettuce leaves***

***3 sliced tomatoes***

***1 1/2 fl oz (40 ml) cocktail sauce***

*Preparation time: approx. 30 minutes*
*Per serving: approx. 310 cals/1302 kj*

**1** Wash, dry and dice the turkey meat. Mince the meat using the medium setting on your mincer. Mix in the salsa sauce.

**2** Crush the tortilla crisps. Wash, dry and finely chop the coriander. Peel and dice the onions. Peel and crush the clove of garlic.

**3** Mix together the meat, tortilla crumbs, coriander, onions and garlic and season with salt, cayenne pepper and the caraway seeds. Wet your hands and make 4 burgers out of the mixture.

**4** Heat the oil in a frying pan and cook the meat on both sides for approximately 8 minutes. Grill the baps. Wash, dry and place the lettuce leaves on the bottom halves of the baps

**5** Place the tomato slices on top and cover with the cooked burgers. Spread on the cocktail sauce, cover with the top halves and serve.

# Light Prawn Sandwich

***4 slices rye bread***

***2 tbsp creamed horseradish***

***7 oz (200 g) prawns***

***2 red onions***

***2 cloves of garlic***

***4 tbsp rice wine***

***3 tbsp soy sauce***

***3 eggs***

***2 fl oz (50 ml) milk***

***salt***

***pepper***

***3 tbsp oil***

***1 sheet nori seaweed***

*Preparation time: approx. 25 minutes*
*Per serving: approx. 291 cals/1223 kj*

**1** Spread the creamed horseradish onto the slices of rye bread. Cut the prawns into bite sized pieces. Peel and dice the onions. Peel and finely chop the cloves of garlic.

**2** Mix together the onions, garlic, rice wine and soy sauce and leave to steep for approximately 10 minutes. In the meantime transfer the eggs and milk into a bowl and mix. Season with salt and pepper.

**3** Heat the oil in a frying pan and cook the scrambled eggs. Roast the nori seaweed sheet in a frying pan without any oil or butter and tear into small pieces.

**4** Pile the prawn mixture onto the slices of rye bread, top with the scrambled egg and sprinkle with the pieces of nori seaweed.

*Eggs keep for up to four weeks in the refrigerator. You can cook or fry them even after the "best before" date. It is very easy to test the freshness of an egg: fill up a glass with cold water and place the egg in it. If it floats it is on the old side, a fresh egg would sink to the bottom.*

# Green Cuisine

*Fresh ingredients all year round – why not make use of the many kinds of vegetables you can get nowadays? You will always find fresh vegetables regardless of the season. Enrich your evening meals with light yet healthy dishes such as celeriac carpaccio, chicory with ham and egg or savoury cucumber salad.*

# Potato Fish Salad

***1 lb (500 g) new potatoes***

***salt***

***1 bunch spring onions***

***5 oz (150 g) snow peas***

***3 tbsp pepper butter***

***13 oz (400 g) mackerel fillets***

***4 tbsp sherry vinegar***

***3 tbsp red wine***

***3 tbsp walnut oil***

***salt***

***freshly milled black pepper***

***1/2 bunch dill***

*Preparation time: approx. 35 minutes*
*Per serving: approx. 431 cals/1812 kj*

**1** Peel the potatoes and cook in slightly salted water for approximately 15 minutes. Clean and wash the spring onions and cut into rings.

**2** Clean, wash and dry the snow peas. Melt the pepper butter in a frying pan and sauté the spring onions and snow peas.

**3** Cut the mackerel fillets into bite sized pieces. Mix together the sherry vinegar, red wine and walnut oil and season with salt and pepper

**4** Wash and dry the dill and pluck off the small twiglets. Drain the potatoes. Leave to cool down and slice them. Arrange the vegetables, the potato slices and fish on plates. Pour the dressing over the salad and decorate with the dill. Serve.

*Oil provides the salad with a special touch. Walnut oil in particular has a mild nutty flavour and is highly thought of in the French cuisine. Together with the light sunflower oil, the dressing attains a special culinary touch.*

# Savoury Cucumber Salad

***1 cucumber***

***1 orange***

***3 1/2 oz (100 g) green and***
***3 1/2 oz (100 g) black grapes***

***5 oz (150 g) rolled fillet of turkey ham***

***juice from 1/2 lemon***

***1 bunch lemon balm***

***1 sprig tarragon***

***3 1/2 fl oz (100 ml) single cream***

***2 tbsp sherry***

***sugar***

***salt***

***freshly milled black pepper***

***2 oz (50 g) pumpkin seeds***

*Preparation time: approx. 30 minutes*
*Per serving: approx. 547 cals/2299 kj*

**1** Wash, dry and halve the cucumber lengthwise. Then slice. Peel the orange, making sure to remove the white pithy skin, too. Cut out the segments using a sharp knife.

**2** Wash, dry and halve the grapes. Deseed. Cut the turkey ham into fine strips. Mix the ingredients together and sprinkle with the lemon juice.

**3** Wash, dry and finely chop the herbs. Make a dressing using the single cream, sherry and the seasonings.

**4** Stir in the herbs, pour over the salad and toss well. Coarsely chop the pumpkin seeds. Arrange the salad and sprinkle with the pumpkin seeds. Serve.

*Fresh herbs are the embodiment of nature and fitness.
They provide something for all our senses.
Their enticing aroma is enough to whet your appetite.
The German writer Goethe loved his classic green sauce
with seven different kinds of fresh herbs.
Why not turn your balcony or back yard
into a herb garden?
You can get seeds in any garden centre.*

# Celeriac Carpaccio

***1 1/2 lbs (750 g) root celeriac***

***approx. 2 pints (1 l) vegetable broth***

***6 tbsp lemon juice***

***5 tbsp pumpkin seed oil***

***2 tbsp sherry vinegar***

***salt***

***freshly milled black pepper***

***1 to 2 tbsp pumpkin seeds***

***7 oz (200 g) Parma ham***

*Preparation time: approx. 15 minutes*
*Per serving: approx. 131 cals/550 kj*

**1** Peel the root celeriac, making sure you keep the greens for decoration. Boil the root in the vegetable broth for approximately 10 to 15 minutes or until tender.

**2** Remove from the pot, quench with cold water and leave to cool down thoroughly. When cold, take the celeriac and cut into thin slices. If available, use an electric slicer for this.

**3** Arrange everything on plates. Mix together the lemon juice, pumpkin seed oil and sherry vinegar and season with salt and pepper. Pour the marinade onto the slices of celeriac.

**4** Coarsely chop the pumpkin seeds and cut the Parma ham into thins strips. Place the strips of ham on top of the celeriac slices and sprinkle with the chopped pumpkin seeds. Decorate with the celeriac leaves and serve.

# Yoghurt and Chickpea Mousse

***1 tin chickpeas 9 oz (280 g)***

***3 cloves of garlic***

***1 tsp caraway seeds***

***1/2 tsp ground coriander***

***1 cucumber***

***salt***

***1/2 bunch coriander***

***2 x 5 oz (150 g) tubs natural yoghurt***

***2 tsp olive oil***

***pepper***

*Preparation time: approx. 15 minutes*
*Per serving: approx. 131 cals/550 kj*

**1** Drain the chickpeas using a sieve. Peel the cloves of garlic and transfer to a blender together with the chickpeas, caraway seeds and ground coriander. Blend to a smooth paste.

**2** Peel, halve, deseed and grate the cucumber. Sprinkle with salt and leave to steep for 10 minutes in a sieve. Wash, dry and finely chop the coriander.

**3** Mix together the olive oil and yoghurt to make a smooth mass and season with salt and pepper.

**4** Add the grated cucumber and chick-pea mousse to the yoghurt, transfer to a serving dish and serve with Turkish bread.

# Crispy Vegetable Platter

***1/2 pint (250 ml) vegetable stock***

***3 1/2 to 5 oz (100 to 150 g) wholemeal rice***

***1 cucumber***

***1 bunch radishes***

***3 carrots***

***4 spring onions***

***4 tbsp raspberry vinegar***

***salt***

***lemon pepper***

***5 tbsp grape seed oil***

***2 oz (50 g) frozen herb mixture***

*Preparation time: approx. 35 minutes*
*Per serving: approx. 346 cals/1554 kj*

**1** Transfer the vegetable stock into a pot and bring to the boil. Add the rice and simmer on a low flame for approximately 20 to 25 minutes. Wash the cucumber and slice thinly.

**2** Wash and thinly slice the horseradish. Keep the leaves for decoration purposes.

**3** Peel the carrots and grate finely. Wash and dry the spring onions and cut into rings. Make a marinade using the raspberry vinegar, salt, pepper, grape seed oil and the herb mixture. Pour over the vegetables and toss well.

**4** Stir the vegetable salad into the rice. Garnish with the horseradish leaves and serve warm.

*Wholemeal or brown rice has the husks removed similar to normal white rice, but the grains have not been polished. This means that the grain is still surrounded by a layer of skin containing vitamins, minerals and roughage. Cooked wholemeal rice has a crunchy consistency and a mild nutty flavour.*

# Lukewarm Romana Salad

*8 oz (250 g) mini Romana lettuce*

*2 sprigs thyme*

*2 tomatoes*

*2 oz (60 g) sliced hazelnuts*

*7 oz (200 g) mozzarella cheese*

*1 French stick*

*3 red onions*

*2 cloves of garlic*

*4 tbsp hazelnut oil*

*salt*

*freshly milled black pepper*

*2 to 3 tbsp maple syrup*

*3 tbsp raspberry vinegar*

*Preparation time: approx. 25 minutes*
*Per serving: approx. 559 cals/2349 kj*

**1** Wash the Romana lettuce and remove the stalk. Quarter the lettuce head. Wash and dry the thyme and pluck the leaves off the sprigs.

**2** Wash the tomatoes. Cut in half and remove the green around the stems. Quarter each half of the tomato. Roast the hazelnuts in a frying pan without oil or butter until they are brown. Dice the mozzarella cheese.

**3** Slice the French stick and toast. Alternatively, roast in a frying pan without oil or butter. Peel and dice the onions and cloves of garlic finely. Heat the peanut oil in a frying pan and sauté the onions and garlic.

**4** Season with salt and pepper and add the maple syrup and the raspberry vinegar. Keep on the flame until hot. Place the lettuce on plates, add the tomatoes and sprinkle with the mozzarella and the sliced hazelnuts. Pour over the warm salad dressing. Sprinkle with the thyme leaves. Arrange the toasted French slices next to the salad and serve.

# Hungarian Letcho with Puffy Cheese

***7 oz frozen Hungarian letcho (vegetable mix)***

***fat to grease the forms***

***2 onions***

***2 tbsp oil***

***salt***

***cayenne pepper***

***2 eggs***

***2 tbsp single cream***

***3 tbsp grated cheddar***

*Preparation time: approx. 25 minutes*
*Per serving: approx. 427 cals/1793 kj*

**1** Place the Hungarian vegetable mix on a sieve and leave to defrost. Preheat the oven to gas mark 6 (400° F or 200° C). Place the defrosted vegetable mix in four small, already greased forms.

**2** Peel and finely dice the onions. Heat the oil in a frying pan and sauté the onions. Spoon them over the vegetable mixture.

**3** Season with salt and pepper. Separate the eggs and whisk the egg whites until firm. Place a bowl into a pot full of barely simmering water and whisk the egg yolks and single cream until the mixture is thick and creamy.

**4** Very carefully stir and fold in the whisked egg whites and the grated cheese into the egg yolk mixture. Transfer the mousse onto the vegetable mix and place in the centre of the oven. Bake for approximately 5 to 10 minutes. Serve the letcho warm.

# Chicory with Ham and Eggs

***10 oz (300 g) chicory***

***7 oz (200 g) ham from the lamb, alternatively Parma ham***

***3 1/2 oz (100 g) cucumber***

***5 oz (150 g) Emmenthal cheese***

***3 eggs***

***1 bunch spring onions***

***1 tbsp sweet mustard***

***lemon juice***

***sugar***

***salt***

***freshly milled black pepper***

***3 tbsp sherry vinegar***

***6 tbsp grape seed oil***

*Preparation time: approx. 35 minutes*
*Per serving: approx. 431 cals/1812 kj*

**1** Wash and dry the chicory. Remove the stem and cut the vegetable into rings. Cut the ham into fine strips.

**2** Wash, dry and cut the cucumber into thin sticks. Grate the cheese finely. Boil the eggs until hard, rinse under running cold water, peel and chop finely. Wash and dry the spring onions and cut into rings.

**3** Make the salad dressing with the mustard, lemon juice, sugar, salt, pepper, sherry vinegar and grape seed oil. Stir in the onion rings.

**4** Mix together the chicory, strips of ham and cucumber sticks and pour over the salad dressing. Sprinkle with the eggs and grated cheese and serve.

*This tasty winter vegetable was discovered more or less by chance at the turn of last century by a Belgian farmer. Their stored chicory roots (a base ingredient for Ersatz coffee) started growing yellowy white sprouts in the spring. They were quite bitter to start off with but selective breeding resulted in chicory which nowadays has attained the status of a delicacy.*

# Pasta Dishes

*You simply cannot do without pasta if you want to cook in the evening. Pasta does not only fill you up, but makes you happy and puts you in a good mood! Carbohydrates in the form of tortellini on spider mustard or an Asian pasta pot are just the thing to get you going again after a long day's work!*

# Tortellini on Young Mustard Greens

***10 oz (300 g) fresh meat filled tortellini from the cooler section in your supermarket***

***10 to 13 oz (300 to 400 g) fresh young mustard greens***

***2 to 3 tbsp olive oil***

***salt***

***freshly milled black pepper***

***1/4 pint (125 ml) chicken stock***

***1 packet ready-made sauce Béarnaise***

*Preparation time: approx. 30 minutes*
*Per serving: approx. 439 cals/1846 kj*

**1** Cook the tortellini following the instructions on the packet. In the meantime wash and dry the young mustard greens and chop coarsely.

**2** Heat the olive oil in a frying pan and add the young mustard greens. Season with salt and pepper, give it a quick stir and add the chicken stock. Cook for approximately 6 to 8 minutes.

**3** Prepare the sauce Béarnaise following the instructions on the packet. Arrange the young mustard greens on plates.

**4** Pour the sauce over the young mustard greens and top with the tortellini. Serve.

*Young mustard greens – a leafy stalk vegetable from beets or seakale has almost been forgotten over time. You should only eat the young leaves – a taste experience well worth it, as it is quite a delicacy if you can get hold of it fresh on a market. Alternatively, substitute it with either spinach or seakale.*

# Pasta Bake

***1 tbsp olive oil***

***2 tbsp lemon juice***

***13 oz (400 g) fettuccine***

***3 1/2 fl oz (100 ml) single cream***

***2 eggs***

***3 1/2 oz (100 g) sugar***

***1 sachet vanilla sugar***

***butter or margerine to grease the oven-proof dish***

***3 1/2 oz (100 g) ground nuts***

***1 tsp cinnamon***

***2 tbsp butter flakes***

*Preparation time: approx. 35 minutes*
*Per serving: approx. 415 cals/1744 kj*

**1** Bring sufficient water to the boil and add the lemon juice and olive oil. Cook the fettuccine until al dente or firm to the bite.

**2** Drain the fettuccine, rinse them under running cold water and put to one side. Mix together the single cream, eggs, half the sugar and the vanilla sugar.

**3** Grease an oven-proof dish with the fat. Preheat the oven to gas mark 6 (400° F or 200° C). Arrange the fettuccine in the oven-proof dish and pour over the egg and cream mixture.

**4** Sprinkle with the cinnamon and the ground nuts. Also, sprinkle the butter flakes on the dish and place in the centre of the oven. Bake for approximately 20 minutes. Take out and serve.

*Leftover pasta is ideal for a quick and inventive meal.*
*This casserole also has a savoury version.*
*Simply leave out the sugar, cinnamon and nuts and replace those ingredients with salt and pepper for seasoning and add some tuna fish.*

# Macaroni with Venison

**12 oz (350 g) macaroni**

**salt**

**14 oz (400 g) frozen venison with sauce**

**2 oz (50 g) small bacon strips**

**1/2 bunch thyme**

**1 sprig rosemary**

**1/2 pint (500 ml) red wine**

**2 tbsp Cumberland sauce**

**2 tbsp sour cream**

**freshly milled black pepper**

**ground allspice**

*Preparation time: approx. 30 minutes*
*Per serving: approx. 377 cals/1583 kj*

1 Bring sufficient water to the boil, add some salt and cook the macaroni until al dente or firm to the bite. Prepare the venison following the instructions on the packet, then dice the meat. Put the sauce aside for the moment.

2 Roast the bacon strips in a frying pan without fat until the bacon is tinged golden brown and the fat has melted. Add the venison. Wash, dry and finely chop the herbs.

3 Add the herbs, venison sauce, red wine and the Cumberland sauce to the meat and cook for approximately 6 to 7 minutes.

4 Stir in the sour cream and season with salt, pepper and the ground allspice or pimento. Drain the macaroni, rinse under running cold water, arrange on plates and top with the meat. Serve.

# Green Tagliatelle with Tomatoes

**8 oz (250 g) green tagliatelle**

**salt**

**10 tomatoes**

**2 green and 2 yellow peppers**

**3 1/2 oz (100 g) onions**

**1 clove of garlic**

**3 oz (80 g) clarified butter**

**freshly milled black pepper**

**1 tbsp chilli sauce**

**1 bunch basil**

**2 to 3 tbsp grated Pecorino cheese**

*Preparation time: approx. 25 minutes*
*Per serving: approx. 327 cals/1375 kj*

**1** Cook the tagliatelle until firm to the bite.Take the tomatoes and make crosswise incisions with a sharp knife, dip into hot water, rinse under the running cold tap and peel off the skin. Cut, deseed and dice the tomatoes.

**2** Wash the peppers and cut in half lengthwise. Deseed and dice. Peel and finely chop the onions and clove of garlic.

**3** Melt the clarified butter in a frying pan and sauté the the onion and garlic. Then add the tomatoes and peppers. Cook for approximately 6 to 8 minutes. Season with salt, pepper and the chilli sauce.

**4** Wash, dry and coarsely chop the basil. Drain the tagliatelle and arrange on plates. Pour over the vegetable mixture and sprinkle with the basil and the Pecorino cheese. Serve.

# Ravioli Bake

***7 oz (200 g) artichoke bottoms***

***8 oz (250 g) mussels pickled with herbs***

***1 fl oz (2 cl) Grappa***

***10 oz (300 g) fresh ravioli filled with vegetables from the cooler section in your supermarket***

***butter or margarine to grease the oven-proof dish***

***3 1/2 oz (100 g) grated Parmesan cheese***

***3 tbsp tomato purée***

***1 to 2 tbsp butter flakes***

*Preparation time: approx. 35 minutes*
*Per serving: approx. 368 cals/1547 kj*

**1** Drain the artichoke bottoms and mussels using a colander. Make sure you catch the herb liquid from the mussels in a bowl and stir in the Grappa. Cook the ravioli following the instructions on the packet.

**2** Grease a shallow oven-proof baking dish with the fat. Preheat the oven to gas mark 4 (350° F or 180° C). Place the artichoke bottoms in the oven-proof dish.

**3** Drain the ravioli, rinse under the running cold tap and leave to dry a little. Then place them on top of the artichoke bottoms. Also add the mussels to the oven-proof dish.

**4** Add the grated Parmesan cheese to the mussel liquid and pour over the oven-proof dish. Sprinkle with the butter flakes and place in the centre of the oven. Bake for approximately 8 to 10 minutes. Serve.

*Pasta from the cooler section is the latest trend among pasta lovers. Ravioli are available with a variety of fillings. You can cook just the amount you need depending on how hungry you are and they are quickly prepared. Also, there is no end to the variety of sauces at your disposal.*

# Asian Pasta Pot

***8 oz (250 g) fillet of pork***

***salt***

***freshly milled black pepper***

***ground mustard seeds and ground ginger***

***3 to 4 tbsp seasoned sesame oil***

***14 oz (400 g) linguine***

***3 1/2 oz (100 g) tinned okra***

***3 1/2 oz (100 g) bamboo shoots***

***2 to 3 tbsp soy sauce***

*Preparation time: approx. 35 minutes*
*Per serving: approx. 341 cals/1434 kj*

**1** Wash and dry the fillet of pork and cut into thin strips. Season with salt, pepper, the ground mustard seeds and ground ginger.

**2** Heat the oil in a frying pan and brown the meat on all sides on a high flame. Put to one side and keep warm. Bring sufficient water to the boil, add some salt and cook the linguine until al dente or firm to the bite.

**3** Drain the okra and bamboo shoots well using a colander and cut into small pieces.

**4** Quickly fry the cooked pasta in the meat juice and the oil still in the frying pan and add the meat and vegetables. Cook for approximately 2 to 3 minutes. Season everything with soy sauce, arrange on plates and serve.

# Pumpkin Spaetzle Gratin

***12 to 13 oz (350 to 400 g) fresh spaetzle (German pasta), salt***

***10 oz (300 g) pickled pumpkin, 7 oz (200 g) tinned lychees, lemon pepper, 1 green pepperoni***

***3 1/2 oz (100 g) frozen peas***

***1/4 pint (125 ml) Asian stock, 3 1/2 fl oz (100 ml) single cream***

***ground ginger and ground cloves***

***butter or margarine to grease the dish***

***5 oz (150 g) grated Appenzeller or Gruyère cheese***

*Preparation time: approx. 35 minutes*
*Per serving: approx. 362 cals/1523 kj*

**1** Cook the spaetzle in sufficient boiling salted water for approximately 5 to 7 minutes. Transfer the pumpkin including the liquid into a pot. Drain the lychees and add to the pumpkin. Also add the peas and put on the heat.

**2** Wash the pepperoni, halve lengthwise, deseed and dice.

**3** Add the pepperoni to the pumpkin mix and simmer on a low flame for approximately 5 minutes. Season well with salt and the spices and add the Asian stock. Continue to cook for another 3 minutes.

**4** Preheat the oven to gas mark 7 (425° F or 220° C). Drain the spaetzle and toss them together with the pumpkin mixture. Grease a shallow oven-proof dish with the fat. Transfer the spaetzle mix into the oven-proof dish. Place in the centre of the oven and bake for approximately 8 minutes or until golden brown. Serve.

# Poultry Dishes

*Quails on sorrel leaves, leg of guinea foul or breast of duck Burgundy style – who says that evening meals cannot be cooked in style? Treat yourself to something special after work – and share it with family and good friends.*

# Quails on Sorrel Leaves

***4 quails, gutted and prepared***

***salt***

***pepper***

***paprika***

***3 tbsp clarified butter***

***1 fl oz (2 cl) port***

***1/2 pint (300 ml) game stock***

***10 oz (300 g) sorrel leaves***

***3 red onions***

***1 clove of garlic***

***nutmeg***

***1 to 2 tbsp maple syrup***

***1 tbsp chopped hazelnuts***

***1 to 2 tbsp sour cream***

*Preparation time: approx. 35 minutes*
*Per serving: approx. 436 cals/1832 kj*

**1** Wash and dry the quails. Season both inside and outside with salt, pepper and paprika. Melt half the clarified butter and brown the quails from all sides on a high flame.

**2** Add the port and half the game stock and leave to simmer on a low flame for approximately 20 to 25 minutes. In the meantime wash and dry the sorrel leaves before chopping them coarsely.

**3** Peel and finely chop the onions and clove of garlic. Melt the remaining clarified butter in a frying pan and sauté the onion and garlic. Add the sorrel leaves and the rest of the game stock.

**4** Leave to simmer on a low flame for approximately 10 minutes. Season the vegetables with salt, pepper and nutmeg. 5 minutes before it is ready brush the maple syrup onto the quails. Roast the hazelnuts in a frying pan without any fat until golden brown. Arrange the sorrel vegetable mixture on plates, place the quail on top and sprinkle with the hazelnuts. Decorate with the sour cream and serve.

*The tasty wild fowl is specially bred these days. In former times one would come across them when going out for a walk in the woods. Quails are available all year round. They are either fresh or frozen and are of excellent quality*

# Sizzling Turkey Delight

***13 oz (400 g) turkey fillet***

***pepper***

***paprika***

***2 onions***

***3 tomatoes***

***3 tbsp clarified butter***

***salt***

***1 to 2 tsp dried sage***

***10 oz (300 g) frozen mixed vegetables***

***5 tbsp chicken stock***

***lemon pepper***

*Preparation time: approx. 25 minutes*
*Per serving: approx. 396 cals/1666 kj*

**1** Wash, dry and slice the turkey fillets. Season with pepper and paprika. Peel and finely chop the onions.

**2** Wash and quarter the tomatoes. Melt half the clarified butter in a frying pan and brown the meat strips on a high flame on all sides. Season with salt and remove from the pan. Put to one side.

**3** Melt the remaining clarified butter in the frying pan and sauté the onions together with the sage. Add the defrosted vegetable mixture and chicken stock.

**4** Season with salt and lemon pepper and add the tomatoes. Leave to simmer on a low flame for approximately 5 to 10 minutes. Add the meat and cook until hot. Arrange on plates and serve.

*Sage is a popular herb in the Mediterranean cuisine. The furry green leaves have a white back and a very intensive, savoury tangy aroma. Sage should therefore be used sparingly. The hardy perennial is also at home in our climate.*

# Leg of Guinea Fowl

***4 guinea fowl legs***

***salt, pepper***

***paprika***

***1 1/2 oz (40 g) pepper butter***

***1 fl oz (2 cl) Calvados***

***3 1/2 fl oz (100 ml) chicken stock***

***1 tin Calvados apples (9 oz/280 g net weight)***

***3 1/2 oz (100 g) frozen herbs Provencal***

***3 1/2 oz (100 g) double cream***

*Preparation time: approx. 40 minutes*
*Per serving: approx. 466 cals/ 1957 kj*

**1** Wash and dry the guinea foul legs. Rub with salt, pepper and paprika from all sides.

**2** Melt the pepper butter in a frying pan and brown the legs on all sides on a high heat. Add the Calvados and chicken stock and leave to simmer on a low flame for approximately 25 minutes.

**3** Add the Calvados apples including the liquid and the defrosted herbs. Cook for a further 5 minutes.

**4** Remove the legs and add the double cream to the pan. Season again if necessary. Arrange the guinea fowl legs and Calvados apples on plates, spoon the sauce on top and serve. A mixture of brown and wild rice makes for an ideal accompaniment to this dish.

*The ancestor of the domestic guinea fowl is from Africa. These days the tasty bird is bred all over the world. Many of the guinea fowls you see in the local supermarket come from France. The tender, dark and lean meat has a distinctive game flavour.*

# Gipsy Liver

***12 to 13 oz (350 to 400 g) chicken liver***

***3 tbsp walnut oil***

***2 onions***

***2 cloves of garlic***

***2 red pepperoni***

***1 yellow pepper***

***2 tbsp tomato purée***

***1/2 pint (250 ml) red wine***

***1 1/2 fl oz (4 cl) Madeira wine***

***salt, pepper***

***paprika***

***1 bunch basil***

***4 to 8 ready-made vol-au-vents***

*Preparation time: approx. 30 minutes*
*Per serving: approx. 399 cals/1677 kj*

**1** Wash, dry and chop the liver into bite sized pieces. Heat the walnut oil in a frying pan and brown on a high flame on all sides.

**2** Peel and finely chop the onions and the cloves of garlic. Wash the pepperoni and peppers and halve lengthwise. Then deseed and chop finely.

**3** Add the pepperoni, peppers, onions and garlic to the liver and sauté while giving it a good stir. Add the tomato purée.

**4** Pour in the red wine and the Madeira wine. Season well with salt, pepper and paprika and leave to simmer on a low flame for approximately 5 minutes. Wash, dry and cut the basil into strips. Heat the vol-au-vents in the oven following the instructions on the packet. Transfer the gipsy liver into the hot vol-au-vents, decorate with the basil and serve .

# Squire's Breast of Goose

***1 packet ready-made dough for potato fritters***

***2 shallots***

***3 1/2 oz (100 g) small bacon strips***

***ground coriander and ground caraway seeds***

***10 oz (300 g) smoked goose breast***

***clarified butter for frying***

***1 oz (20 g) truffles***

***5 tbsp yoghurt***

***2 to 3 tbsp truffle oil***

***2 tbsp chopped tarragon***

***2 to 3 tbsp white port***

*Preparation time: approx. 35 minutes*
*Per serving: approx. 456 cals/1915 kj*

**1** Prepare the dough for the potato fritters following the instructions on the packet. Peel and finely dice the shallots. Roast the bacon in a frying pan without any oil or butter until the fat has melted.

**2** Fold the bacon strips and shallots under the fritter dough and season with the ground coriander and ground caraway seeds.

**3** Slice the breast of goose very thinly. Melt the clarified butter in a frying pan and cook the potato fritters. Place the cooked fritters on kitchen towels to absorb any excess fat and arrange on plates.

**4** Place the goose slices on top of the potato fritters and sprinkle with the grated truffle. Mix together the yoghurt, truffle oil, tarragon and port. Serve the dip in a separate small dish.

# Chicken Gnocchi Gratin

***2 lbs (1 kg) frozen broccoli***

***salt***

***1/2 oz (10 g) frozen Italian herbs***

***7 oz (200 g) smoked chicken breast***

***13 oz (400 g) fresh ready-made gnocchi***

***4 tbsp olive oil***

***pepper***

***butter or margarine to grease the oven-proof dish***

***3 1/2 oz (100 g) mild cheddar***

*Preparation time: approx. 30 minutes*
*Per serving: approx. 392 cals/1648 kj*

**1** Cook the broccoli in a little salted water for approximately 8 to 10 minutes. Then remove from the hob and drain using a sieve. Carefully mix in the defrosted Italian herbs.

**2** Finely slice the chicken breast. Heat the olive oil in a frying pan and cook the gnocchi for approximately 2 to 3 minutes. Add the broccoli and chicken strips. Season with salt and pepper.

**3** Grease a shallow oven-proof dish with the fat. Preheat the oven to gas mark 7 (440° F or 220° C). Spoon the gnocchi mixture into the oven-proof dish and gratethe cheese on top. Place in the centre of the oven and bake for approximately 15 minutes. Serve.

*This dish is also lovely if you use spaetzle or other fresh pasta available from the cooling section in your local supermarket.*

# Breast of Duck Burgundy Style

***2 breast of duck fillets (boned, with skin)***

***salt***

***pepper***

***3 1/2 oz (100g) frozen herbs Provencal***

***3 tbsp olive oil***

***7 fl oz (200 ml) red wine***

***13 oz (400 g) frozen French vegetable mix***

*Preparation time: approx. 20 minutes*
*Per serving: approx.490 cals/2060 kj*

**1** Wash and dry the duck fillets and season with salt and pepper. Rub in the defrosted herbs. Heat the olive oil in a frying pan and brown the meat from all sides for about 8 to 10 minutes.

**2** Add the red wine and vegetables and continue to simmer on a low flame for a further 5 to 10 minutes.

**3** Remove the duck breast, slice and keep warm.

**4** Leave the French vegetables to cook properly. Arrange the meat on plates, add the vegetables and serve. Rice makes for an ideal accompaniment to this dish.

*To get a really juicy breast of duck you should score the skin with cross-cross cuts using a sharp knife. Brown on both sides in a frying pan and place, with the skin facing you, in a baking tray on the middle shelf in the oven on gas mark 4 (350° F or 180° C) for approximately 12 to 15 minutes.*

# Meat Dishes

*Meat is especially satisfying because it is prepared so quickly. These meat dishes will add some zest to your life and finesse to your evenings at home. Try tender fillets of lamb, paillards with basil or rump steak in orange sauce.*

# Exotic Fillet of Hare

**1 1/4 lbs (600 g) fillet of hare**

**7 oz (200 g) shiitake mushrooms**

**3 1/2 oz (100 g) tinned bamboo sprouts**

**1 fl oz (2 cl) sherry**

**2 tbsp soy sauce**

**1 tbsp tomato purée**

**ground ginger, ground mustard seeds, ground caraway seeds and ground garlic**

**salt**

**pepper**

**3 to4 tbsp peanut oil**

**glass noodles as accompaniment**

*Preparation time: approx. 20 minutes (plus steeping time)*
*Per serving: approx. 393 cals/1652 kj*

**1** Wash, dry and dice the fillet of hare. Wash and dry the shiitake mushrooms.

**2** Drain the bamboo sprouts well using a sieve. Mix together the sherry, soy sauce, tomato purée and the seasonings.

**3** Mix together the diced fillet of hare, shiitake mushrooms and the bamboo sprouts and transfer into the sauce. Marinade for approximately 30 to 45 minutes.

**4** Heat the peanut oil in a frying pan and fry the meat and vegetables for roughly 10 to 15 minutes. Arrange the fillet of hare with the vegetables and glass noodles on plates and serve.

*Asian seasonings will lend all game a special note. You can also use venison or roe for this dish, be it a fillet or goulash. If you decide on the latter you may have to cook it a little longer.*

# Mixed Pickles Goulash

***1 1/4 lbs (600 g) tinned beef goulash***

***1 lb (500 g) mixed pickles***

***7 oz (200 g) tinned asparagus***

***1 1/2 fl oz (4 cl) port***

***4 to 5 tbsp double cream***

***1 bunch parsley***

*Preparation time: approx. 20 minutes*
*Per serving: approx. 463 cals/1945 kj*

**1** Heat the beef goulash carefully. Drain the mixed pickles and asparagus using a sieve.

**2** Add the vegetables and port to the meat. Heat on a low flame while stirring continuously.

**3** Stir in the double cream. Wash, dry and finely chop the parsley. Transfer the goulash onto plates and decorate with the parsley. Rice makes for an ideal accompaniment to this dish.

# Quick Smoked Pork Chop

***13 oz (400 g) small potatoes***

***13 oz (400 g) smoked pork chop, boned***

***2 onions***

***1 clove of garlic***

***2 tbsp clarified butter***

***1/2 pint (250 ml) real ale***

***1 tsp caraway seeds***

***salt***

***coarsely milled black pepper***

***1/4 bunch thyme***

***basil for decoration***

*Preparation time: approx. 25 minutes*
*Per serving: approx. 439 cals/1846 kj*

**1** Peel and cook the potatoes. Slice the smoked pork chops into strips as thick as a finger. Peel and finely chop the onions and clove of garlic.

**2** Drain and finely dice the potatoes. Heat the clarified butter in a frying pan and sauté the onions and garlic until they are transparent.

**3** Add the potatoes and strips of smoked pork chop and cook for approximately 5 to 10 minutes. Pour in the real ale and season with salt, pepper and the caraway seeds. Leave to simmer on a low flame for a further 5 to 10 minutes.

**4** Wash and dry the thyme. Pluck the leaves off the sprigs. Arrange the meat on plates and decorate with the thyme leaves. Serve.

# Paillards with Basil

***8 very thin escalopes of veal***

***salt***

***pepper***

***1 to 2 tbsp clarified butter***

***1 bunch basil***

***2 fl oz (6 cl) Madeira wine***

***3 to 4 tbsp chopped tomatoes***

***1 tbsp lemon zest***

***basil for decoration***

*Preparation time: approx. 30 minutes*
*Per serving: approx. 417 cals/1754 kj*

**1** Wash, dry and season the escalopes of veal with salt and pepper. Melt the clarified butter in a frying pan and brown the meat on both sides for 3 to 4 minutes. Remove and put to one side. Keep warm.

**2** Wash and dry the basil. Pluck the leaves off the stems. Quickly fry the basil leaves in the remaining fat in the frying pan.

**3** Add the Madeira wine and chopped tomatoes and cook on a low flame for approximately 5 minutes.

**4** Season the sauce with salt and pepper. Arrange the paillards on plates and pour over the sauce. Decorate with the lemon zest and basil and serve.

*Paillards are very thinly sliced escalopes and therefore require just a short time in the frying pan. You can ask you butcher to cut them for you or, if you want to cut them yourself, place the meat in the freezer for half an hour or so before you set the knife or preferably a food slicer to it.*

# Asparagus and Ham Wraps

***7 oz (200 g) green asparagus***

***1 pint (500 ml) game stock***

***13 oz (400 g) thinly sliced venison ham***

***7 oz (200 g) yoghurt***

***1 to 2 tbsp double cream***

***1 tbsp finely crushed juniper berries***

***1 1/2 fl oz (2 cl) gin***

*Preparation time: approx. 25 minutes*
*Per serving: approx. 288 cals/1211 kj*

**1** Clean and cook the asparagus stalks in the simmering game stock for approximately 15 to 20 minutes. Remove and leave to dry.

**2** Place the ham onto your working surface. Mix together the yoghurt, double cream, juniper berries and gin.

**3** Spread the yoghurt mixture onto the slices of ham and top with the asparagus. Roll everything into wraps and serve. A French stick makes for an ideal accompaniment to this dish.

# Filled Ring of Sausage

***1 red pepper***

***1 tbsp butter***

***10 oz (300 g) sauerkraut***

***1 oz (20 g) pepper butter***

***1 1/2 lbs (700 g) Polish ring sausage***

***1/2 pint (300 ml) milk***

***salt, pepper, nutmeg***

***1 sachet ready-made mashed potatoes***

***5 oz (150 g) soft goat's cheese***

***1/2 bunch parsley***

*Preparation time: approx. 25 minutes*
*Per serving: approx. 417 cals/1753 kj*

**1** Wash and halve the pepper lengthwise, then deseed and dice. Melt the butter in a frying pan and sauté the pepper together with the sauerkraut for approximately 10 minutes.

**2** Grease an oven-proof dish.. Preheat the oven to gas mark 7 (445° F or 225° C). Place the sausage into the dish and score the surface with a knife. Add approx. 1/2 pint (250 ml) water, salt, pepper and the nutmeg to the milk and bring to the boil.

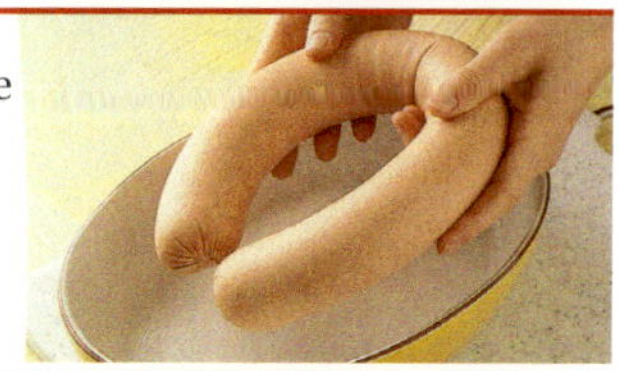

**3** Add the purée mixture and whisk well. Place the mashed potatoes in the middle of the oven-proof dish. Remove the sauerkraut from the pan, drain using a sieve and spoon over the potatoes. Dice the goat's cheese and sprinkle on top.

**4** Place in the centre of the oven and bake for approximately 10 minutes. Wash, dry and finely chop the parsley and sprinkle on top. Serve.

# Rump Steak in Orange Sauce

***4 rump steaks (6 to 7 oz/180 to 200 g each)***

***3 to 4 tbsp peanut oil***

***1/2 pint (250 ml) orange juice***

***2 tbsp thick-cut marmalade***

***1 to 2 tbsp green peppercorns***

***1 tbsp orange liqueur***

***2 to 3 tbsp sour cream***

***salt***

***pepper***

*Preparation time: approx. 20 minutes*
*Per serving: approx. 472 cals/1983 kj*

**1** Wash and dry the steaks. Score the fatty rind a few times with a sharp knife. Heat the peanut oil in a frying pan and sear the steaks on a high flame for approximately 1 minute on each side.

**2** Continue to fry the steaks on a medium flame according to taste. Remove the meat and wrap in aluminium foil to keep warm.

**3** Add the marmalade and green peppercorns and continue to cook for a further 3 to 5 minutes. Season with the orange liqueur and stir in the sour cream.

**4** Take the steaks out of the foil, season with salt and pepper and arrange on plates. Pour on the sauce and serve. Potato croquettes make for an ideal accompaniment to this dish.

*Place the steaks into a very hot frying pan in order to close the pores immediately. It is also important that all meats that have a fatty rind have this scored before frying to prevent the rind from arching.*

# Tender Fillets of Lamb

***13 oz (400 g) fillet of lamb***

***4 tbsp garlic oil***

***salt***

***cayenne pepper***

***1 to 2 cloves of garlic***

***3 1/2 oz (100 g) frozen Italian herbs***

***2 sprigs rosemary***

***1 1/2 fl oz (4 cl) ouzo***

***Turkish bread and tzatziki as accompaniment***

*Preparation time: approx. 20 minutes*
*Per serving: approx. 300 cals/ 1260 kj*

**1** Wash, dry and thinly slice the fillets of lamb. Mix together the garlic oil, salt and cayenne pepper.

**2** Peel and finely chop the cloves of garlic and add to the oil mixture. Also add the defrosted Italian herbs and mix well.

**3** Wash and dry the rosemary. Pluck the leaves off the stems, chop finely and add to the oil mixture.

**4** Brush the slices of lamb with the oil mixture and leave to steep for a little while. Fry in a non-stick frying pan for approximately 4 to 5 minutes on all sides.

**5** Set fire to the ouzo and pour it over the meat. Arrange with the Turkish bread and the tzatziki on plates and serve.

# Fish and Seafood

*Fish does not only taste wonderful but is also cooked in a jiffy. Moreover, it is healthy and light. Dive into a world of uncountable possibilities. On the following pages we recommend zander with artichokes, ling with citrus fruits or halibut with honey crust.*

# Zander with Artichokes

***10 oz (300 g) vegetables (any combination of carrots, leeks, swede, celery and onions)***

***1 lime***

***2 tsp black peppercorns and 2 tsp allspice***

***salt***

***2 to 3 sprigs thyme***

***4 zander fillets (7 oz/200 g each)***

***10 oz (300 g) artichoke hearts***

***2 to 3 tbsp walnut oil***

***lemon pepper***

*Preparation time: approx. 20 minutes*
*Per serving: approx. 248 cals/1041 kj*

1 Wash, dry and chop the vegetables and add to a shallow pot with approx. 2 pints (1 l) water. Add 2 slices of lime, the seasonings and the thyme sprigs. Bring everything to the boil.

2 Wash the fillets of fish and add to the stock. Leave to simmer on a low flame for approximately 4 to 5 minutes. Drain the artichoke hearts using a sieve.

**3** Arrange the artichoke hearts on plates, sprinkle with the walnut oil and lemon pepper.

**4** Remove the fish fillets from the stock, add to the plates and decorate with the slices of lime. Serve.

*Continue to simmer the stock for approximately 10 minutes. Pour through a sieve and freeze in small portions. It is an ideal base for other fish recipes.*

# Ling with Citrus Fruits

***4 slices fillet of ling (7 to 8 oz/200 to 250 g each)***

***1 tbsp lemon juice***

***salt, pepper***

***3 oz (80 g) ready-made pepper butter***

***7 oz (200 g) tangerine segments***

***3 1/2 oz (100 g) cumquats***

***1/4 pint (125 ml) grapefruit juice***

***1 to 2 tbsp crème fraîche***

***1 tbsp orange liqueur***

*Preparation time: approx. 25 minutes*
*Per serving: approx. 414 cals/1741 kj*

1 Wash and dry the fillets of ling. Sprinkle with the lemon juice. Season with salt and pepper. Melt the pepper butter in a frying pan and brown the fish from both sides.

2 Remove the fillets, set aside and keep warm. Peel the tangerines and remove the segments or in the case of tinned fruit leave to drain using a sieve. Wash and slice the cumquats.

3 Add the grapefruit juice together with the fruit to the fat in the frying pan and leave to cook on a medium flame for approximately 3 to 4 minutes.

4 Stir in the crème fraîche and add a special touch with the orange liqueur. Arrange the fish on plates, add the sauce and serve. Potato croquettes make for an ideal accompaniment to this dish.

# Mussels and Fennel Ragout

***2 fennel bulbs***

***3 tbsp olive oil***

***3 1/2 oz (100 g) onions***

***1 clove of garlic***

***13 oz (400 g) preserved clams***

***1/4 pint (150 ml) fish stock***

***1 tsp crab butter***

***2 to 3 tbsp ready-made sauce Béarnaise***

*Preparation time: approx. 20 minutes*
*Per serving: approx. 252 cals/1060 kj*

**1** Clean the fennel bulbs and remove the green leaves, keeping them on one side. Wash and dry the bulbs and cut into strips. Peel and finely chop the onions and clove of garlic.

**2** Heat the oil in a frying pan and sauté the onions and garlic. Add the fennel and cook for approximately 3 to 4 minutes.

**3** Drain the clams using a sieve and add to the vegetables. Add the fish stock and cook on a low flame for approximately 2 to 3 minutes.

**4** Carefully stir in the crab butter and sauce Béarnaise. Arrange on plates and decorate with the fennel leaves. Rice makes for an ideal accompaniment to this dish.

# Stewed Seafood

**1 1/2 lbs (750 g) frozen seafood mix**

**lemon juice**

**butter or margarine to grease the oven-proof dish**

**3 1/2 oz (100 g) onions**

**1 clove of garlic**

**3 1/2 oz (100 g) mild preserved pepperoni**

**3 1/2 oz (100 g) tomato purée**

**2 oz (50 g) frozen Italian herbs**

**1/4 pint (125 ml) red wine**

**salt**

**pepper**

*Preparation time: approx. 30 minutes*
*Per serving: approx. 259 cals/1090 kj*

1 Defrost the seafood following the instructions on the packet. Preheat the oven to gas mark 4 (350° F or 180° C). Sprinkle the seafood with the lemon juice and place in an already greased oven-proof dish.

2 Sprinkle with chopped onions and garlic. Drain the pepperoni using a sieve and dice. Add to the oven-proof dish together with the tomato purée.

3 Mix together the defrosted herbs and the red wine and pour over the food. Season everything with salt and pepper.

4 Place in the centre of the oven and bake for approximately 10 to 15 minutes. Arrange on plates and serve.

*Why not serve a home-made garlic bread with this dish? All you have to do is cut a small French stick into slices and toast or roast them in a frying pan. Then spread on garlic butter or rub with half a clove of garlic.*

# Eel and Cucumber Platter

**1 1/4 lbs (600 g) fillet of eel**

**4 to 5 tbsp sesame oil, salt, pepper**

**1 cucumber**

**3 1/2 oz (100 g) onions**

**2 to 3 tbsp chilli sauce**

**1/2 pint (250 ml) unsweetened coconut milk**

**2 tbsp desiccated coconut**

**ground curcuma, ground coriander and ground ginger**

*Preparation time: approx. 20 minutes*
*Per serving: approx. 202 cals/849 kj*

1 Wash and dry the fillet of eel and cut into thin strips. Heat the sesame oil in a frying pan and fry the fish from all sides. Season with salt and pepper. Peel and dice the onions.

2 Peel and finely dice the cucumber and add to the frying pan. Also add the onions, chilli sauce and coconut milk. Leave to simmer on a low flame for approximately 3 to 4 minutes.

3 Stir in the desiccated coconut and season with the ground curcuma, coriander and ginger. Arrange on plates and serve. A French stick makes for an ideal accompaniment to this dish.

# Halibut with Honey Crust

***4 fillets of halibut (7 oz/200 g each)***

***3 to 4 tbsp honey***

***2 tbsp tomato purée***

***4 to 5 tbsp peanut oil***

***2 to 3 tbsp soy sauce***

***1 tbsp red pepper purée***

***ground ginger, caraway seeds, mustard seeds and cloves***

***10 oz (300 g) frozen Chinese vegetable mix***

*Preparation time: approx. 25 minutes*
*Per serving: approx. 458 cals/1923 kj*

1 Wash and dry the fish fillets. Mix together the honey, the tomato and the pepper purée, soy sauce and seasonings.

2 Brush the fish fillets with the marinade and leave to steep for a short while. Heat the peanut oil in a frying pan and fry the fish on all sides for approximately 6 to 8 minutes or until done.

3 Prepare the frozen Chinese vegetable mix following the instructions on the packet. Arrange the fish on plates, add the vegetables and serve.

# Prawn Ragout

***3 1/2 oz (100 g) 5-minute rice***

***salt***

***7 oz (200 g) okra***

***3 red pepperoni***

***2 celery stalks***

***4 to 5 tbsp peanut oil***

***3 1/2 oz (100 g) onions***

***1 clove of garlic***

***1 pint (100 ml) fish or lobster stock***

***7 oz (200 g) cooked prawns***

***7 oz (200 g) crab sticks***

***1 tbsp lemon juice***

***cayenne pepper***

***Tabasco sauce***

*Preparation time: approx. 25 minutes*
*Per serving: approx. 311 cals/1308 kj*

1 Prepare the rice in slightly salted water following the instructions on the packet. Wash and drain the okra using a colander.

2 Wash the pepperoni, halve lengthwise, deseed and cut into thin strips. Wash and finely dice the celery stalks. Peel and finely chop the onions and the clove of garlic.

3 Heat the oil in a frying pan and sauté the onions and garlic until transparent. Add the okra, celery and pepperoni and cook everything for approximately 4 to 5 minutes.

4 Pour in the fish stock and bring to the boil. Add the cooked prawns. Cut the crab sticks into bite sized pieces and add also. Simmer on a low flame for a further 3 to 4 minutes.

5 Season with lemon juice, cayenne pepper, salt and Tabasco sauce. Stir in the rice, arrange on plates and serve.

# Sardines with Tomato Purée

***1 1/2 lbs (700 g) cleaned and gutted sardines***

***flour***

***3 to 4 tbsp peanut oil***

***2 large onions***

***2 to 3 tbsp olive oil***

***7 oz (200 g) peeled tomatoes***

***3 to 4 tbsp red wine***

***2 oz (50 g) frozen herb mixture***

***salt***

***pepper***

***sugar***

*Preparation time: approx. 30 minutes*
*Per serving: approx. 433 cals/1820 kj*

1 Wash and dry the sardines and dip into the flour. Heat the peanut oil in a frying pan and brown the sardines from all sides for approximately 10 to 12 minutes.

2 Peel and dice the onions. Heat the olive oil in a frying pan and sauté the onions. Add the peeled tomatoes and cook for approximately 2 to 3 minutes.

3 Mash everything lightly with a fork and add the red wine and the defrosted herb mixture. Continue to simmer on a low flame for a further 5 to 6 minutes for the liquid to reduce a little.

4 Season the purée with salt, pepper and sugar. Arrange on plates, place the sardines on top and serve with slices of bread.

*Pita bread is ideal for this dish. You cut it open, put it in the oven, cover both sides with tomato purée and place the fried sardines on top.*

# Light Three-Course Meals

*You have guests coming but are still unclear as to what you are going to cook? On the following pages we will present you with a few light and simple three-course meals that you can dish up any time – even after a long hard day at the office. And they will leave you with enough time to relax and enjoy your evening with your guests.*

# English Three-Course Dinner

## Mussel Soup

**1 lb (500 g) tinned mussel meat**

**2 pints (1 l) fish stock**

**1 fl oz (2 cl) Genever (Dutch gin)**

**1 to 2 tbsp curry powder**

**1 to 2 tbsp crème fraîche**

**2 egg yolks**

*Preparation time: approx. 15 minutes*
*Per serving: approx. 166 cals/699 kj*

1 Drain the mussel meat using a sieve. Heat the fish stock in a pan, add the mussels and keep on the flame for approximately 2 to 3 minutes.

2 Add the Genever and the curry powder and continue to simmer on a low flame for a further 2 to 3 minutes.

3 Stir the crème fraîche into the soup and thicken with the egg yolks. Transfer to soup plates and serve.

## Tea Mousse

**1/4 pint (125 ml) yogi tea (available in a well-stocked health food shop)**

**13 oz (400 g) yoghurt**

**2 to 3 tbsp maple syrup**

*Preparation time: approx. 15 minutes*
*Per serving: approx. 167 cals/ 701 kj*

1 Brew the yogi tea following the instructions on the packet and leave to cool.

2 Mix together the cold tea and yoghurt. Sweeten with the maple syrup and serve in dessert bowls.

## Gourmet-Toast

**4 slices wholemeal toast**

**3 1/2 oz (100 g) butter**

**4 small pork steaks (7 oz/200 g each)**

**salt**

**pepper**

**7 oz (200 g) tinned mixed mushrooms**

**1 1/2 fl oz (4 cl) brandy**

**4 slices Chester cheese**

*Preparation time: approx. 30 minutes*
*Per serving: approx. 567 cals/2381 kj*

1 Melt 2 oz (50 g) of butter in a frying pan and roast the slices of bread on both sides. Wash and dry the pork steaks. Melt the remaining butter in the frying pan and brown the steaks on both sides for approximately 3 to 5 minutes. Season with salt and pepper. Remove and keep warm.

2 Drain the tinned mixed mushrooms using a sieve. Transfer to the frying pan and cook for approximately 3 to 5 minutes in the remaining fat. Pour the brandy over the mushrooms.

3 Preheat the oven to gas mark 7 (440° F or 220° C). Place the steaks on the slices of toast and top with the mushrooms. Cover each one with a slice of Chester cheese.

4 Place the toasts on the top shelf in the oven and bake for approximately 8 minutes or until golden brown. Arrange on plates and serve.

# Light Three-Course Dinner

## Goat's Cheese Rolls

***8 oz (250 g) goat's cheese***

***2 oz (50 g) butter***

***3 1/2 fl oz (100 ml) red wine***

***1 red onion***

***1 bunch parsley***

***1 bunch chives***

***paprika***

***pepper***

***4 tbsp chilli sauce***

***4 brown rolls***

*Preparation time: approx. 15 minutes*
*Per serving: approx. 291 cals/ 1222 kj*

1 Mash the goat's cheese with a fork and mix together with the butter and the red wine.

2 Peel the onions and dice finely. Wash, dry and finely chop the herbs. Add both to the goat's cheese and mix thoroughly.

3 Season with paprika, pepper and chilli sauce. Slice the rolls in half and spread with the goat's cheese mixture. Serve.

## Asian Soup Pot

***13 oz (400 g) frozen Chinese vegetable mix***

***2 pints (1 l) Asian stock***

***7 oz (200 g) grilled breast of turkey***

***2 to 3 tbsp soy sauce***

***1/2 tbsp ground 5-spice mixture***

***2 to 3 tbsp sweet and sour pickled ginger***

*Preparation time: approx. 30 minutes*
*Per serving: approx. 145 cals/612 kj*

1 Prepare the frozen Chinese vegetable mix following the instructions on the packet. Add the Asian stock and simmer on a low flame for approximately 4 to 5 minutes.

2 Dice the turkey breast and add to the pan. Season everything with the soy sauce and the 5-spice mixture.

3 Drain the pickled ginger using a sieve, slice and transfer to soup plates. Pour the soup on top and serve.

## Fruit Kefir

***2 to 3 bananas***

***13 oz (400 g) preserved black currants***

***1 fl oz (2 cl) Batida de Coco or coconut milk***

***1 tbsp vanilla sugar***

***1 pinch ground aniseed***

***1 lb (500 g) kefir or buttermilk***

*Preparation time: approx. 10 minutes*
*Per serving: approx. 197 cals/827 kj*

1 Peel the bananas and cut into largish pieces. Drain the black currents using a sieve.

2 Mix together with the Batida de Coco or the coconut milk, vanilla sugar and ground aniseed and blend.

3 Stir in the kefir or buttermilk, transfer to dessert bowls and serve.

# Last Minute Three-Course Meal

## Delicate Mushroom Broth

***2 oz (50 g) small bacon strips***

***7 oz (200 g) chanterelle mushrooms***

***2 oz (50 g) onions***

***1 clove of garlic***

***2 oz (50 g) chopped parsley***

***2 pints (1 l) mushroom stock***

***1 fl oz (2 cl) herbal liqueur***

*Preparation time: approx. 20 minutes*
*Per serving: approx. 98 cals/411 kj*

1 Roast the bacon strips in a large pot until the fat starts to melt. In the meantime clean the chanterelle mushrooms. Peel and finely chop the onions and clove of garlic.

2 Add the chanterelle mushrooms, onions and garlic to the bacon strips and sauté for approximately 2 to 3 minutes, stirring all the time.

3 Add the parsley and mushroom stock. Bring to the boil and season with the herbal liqueur. Transfer onto soup plates and serve.

## Ice Cream with Fruits of the Forest

***10 oz (300 g) frozen fruits of the forest***

***1 tbsp brown sugar***

***2 fl oz (6 cl) Madeira wine***

***8 scoops vanilla ice cream***

*Preparation time: approx. 10 minutes*
*Per serving: approx. 422 cals/1772 kj*

1 Mix together the fruits of the forest mix, the Madeira wine and sugar and simmer on a low flame for approximately 5 to 6 minutes

2 Arrange the fruits on dessert plates, add the ice cream and serve.

## Russian Potato Salad

***10 oz (300 g) boiled potatoes out of the glass***

***7 oz (200 g) sliced cooked***

***beetroot out of the glass***

***3 1/2 oz (100 g) cornichons***

***3 1/2 fl oz (100 ml) vegetable stock***

***2 to 3 tbsp raspberry vinegar***

***2 to 3 tbsp hazelnut oil***

***salt, pepper***

***8 oz (250 g) smoked sturgeon fillets***

***1 to 2 tbsp keta caviar***

*Preparation time: approx. 40 minutes*
*Per serving: approx. 220 cals/ 924 kj*

1 Drain the potatoes, beetroot and cornichons using a sieve. Finely dice everything.

2 Mix together the vegetable stock with the hazelnut oil and the raspberry vinegar and add to the vegetables. Leave the salad to steep for approximately 20 minutes and arrange on plates.

3 Cut the smoked sturgeon fillets into strips and arrange on the salad. Decorate with the caviar and serve.

# Savoury Three-Course Dinner

## Marinated Celeriac

***13 oz (400 g) celeriac***

***1/2 pint (250 ml) vegetable stock***

***3 tbsp sherry vinegar***

***2 to 3 tbsp oil***

***salt***

***pepper***

***1 pinch ground allspice***

***8 juniper berries***

***1 tsp mustard seeds***

***1/2 lollo rosso lettuce***

***2 to 3 tomatoes***

*Preparation time: approx. 15 minutes*
*Per serving: approx. 158 cals/663 kj*

**1** Peel the celeriac and slice thinly. Bring the vegetable stock to the boil and add the oil, vinegar and seasonings. Simmer on a low heat for approximately 10 minutes.

**2** Remove the celeriac, drain using a sieve and leave to cool. Wash and dry the lollo rosso lettuce and place the leaves on the plates.

**3** Wash, dry and slice the tomatoes. Alternately place the slices of celeriac and tomatoes on the plates, season with salt and pepper and serve.

## Dover Sole with Champagne Mousse

***4 to 6 fillets of Dover sole (6 oz/180 g each)***

***2 to 3 tbsp butter***

***salt***

***pepper***

***1/2 pint (250 ml) red sparkling wine or champagne***

***5 oz (150 g) sour cream***

***1 bunch tarragon***

*Preparation time: approx. 20 minutes*
*Per serving: approx. 317 cals/ 1331 kj*

**1** Wash and dry the fillets of Dover sole. Melt the butter in a frying pan and brown the fish for approximately 3 to 4 minutes on either side. Season, remove from the frying pan and keep warm.

**2** Add the sparkling wine or champagne to the juices in the frying pan and bring to the boil. Stir in the sour cream and season with salt and pepper.

**3** Wash, dry and finely chop the tarragon. Arrange the fillets of Dover sole on plates and add the champagne mousse. Decorate with the tarragon and serve.

## Savoury Pumpkin Mousse

***7 oz (200 g) sweet and sour pickled pumpkin***

***ground cinnamon, ground cloves***

***lemon pepper***

***2 tbsp lemon marmalade***

***8 oz (250 g) cream cheese***

*Preparation time: approx. 10 minutes*
*Per serving: approx. 151 cals/637 kj*

**1** Drain the pickled pumpkin using a sieve. Mash with a fork and season with the spices.

**2** Mix together the lemon marmalade and the cream cheese. Stir in the pickled pumpkin and mix well. Arrange in dessert bowls and serve.

# Desserts

*Feasting without limits. Our grape and soured milk dessert or the apple blackberry mousse will leave you wanting for nothing. And all that without having to feel as though you overindulge. Instead of too many calories all you will find is top taste. Just the ticket to see out a relaxing evening.*

# Grape and Soured Milk Desser

*1 lb (500 g) black grapes*

*1 lb (500 g) soured milk*

*1/2 pint (250 ml) black grape juice*

*1/4 pint (125 ml) Grenadine*

*ground cardamom, ground ginger, ground cloves and ground aniseed*

*2 oz (50 g) candied ginger*

*Preparation time: approx. 15 minutes*
*Per serving: approx. 236 cals/993 kj*

**1** Wash and dry the black grapes. Halve and deseed. Mix together the soured milk, grape juice and the Grenadine.

**2** Add the spices to the soured milk mixture and stir in the black grape halves. Finely chop the ginger.

**3** Transfer the dessert into dessert bowls and sprinkle with the candied ginger. Serve.

*Grapes are rich in vitamins B and C and minerals such as potassium and calcium. Furthermore, the grape sugar is quickly absorbed by the body and turned into energy. Because of their high nutritional value grapes are held in high esteem and considered healthy.*

# Buttermilk Shake

***2 pints (1 l) buttermilk***

***8 oz (250 g) fresh or frozen exotic fruits***

***2 to 3 tbsp honey***

***2 to 3 tbsp single cream***

***1 sachet frozen herb mixture***

***2 to 3 tbsp tomato juice***

***2 to 3 tbsp crème fraîche***

***1 tbsp creamed horse-radish***

***celery stalks for decoration***

*Preparation time: approx. 10 minutes*
*Per serving: approx. 232 cals/975 kj*

**1** Transfer the buttermilk, the lightly defrosted fruits, the honey and the cream to a bowl and blend with a hand-mixeruntil smooth.

**2** Stir the herbs, tomato juice, crème fraîche and creamed horseradish into the buttermilk.

**3** Transfer the buttermilk shake into glasses, decorate with the celery stalks and serve.

*Buttermilk shakes with fruit and herbs are great to quench your thirst. And they are healthy, too. During the summer you should serve this fitness drink thoroughly chilled.*

# Multivitamin Quark

***1 lb (500 g) low fat quark (skimmed-milk soft cheese)***

***2 tbsp double cream***

***10 oz (300 g) morello cherries out of the glass***

***1 pint (500 ml) multifruit juice***

***1/2 bunch lemon balm***

***3 to 4 tbsp cracked wheat***

*Preparation time: approx. 15 minutes*
*Per serving: approx. 404 cals/1697 kj*

**1** Mix together the double cream and the low fat quark until smooth. Drain the cherries using a colander.

**2** Then put the fruit in a blender and blend until smooth. Fold into the quark mixture. Add the multifruit juice and give it a good stir.